EVERYDAY SCIENCE

in the kitchen

Barbara Taylor

photography by

Peter Millard

MACDONALD YOUNG BOOKS

First published in 1995
by Macdonald Young Books Ltd
Campus 400
Maylands Avenue
Hemel Hempstead
Hertfordshire HP2 7EZ

Commissioning editor: Debbie Fox

Project editor: Caroline Wilson

Design: The Design Works, Reading

Illustrators: David Pattison, Geoff Pike

The publisher and author would like to thank Carol Olivier of Kenmont Primary School, and the following children for taking part in the photography: Danny Botross, Marissa Clarke, Nico Codner, Natalie Gashi, Robert Hazell, Rhomaine Hewitt, Samantha Wallace and Melissa Whyte.

Thanks also to Elaine Tanner, Wendy Bray and Angela Bickerton and their classes at St James' Primary School.

Printed and Bound in Portugal by:
Edições ASA

A CIP catalogue record for this book is available from the British Library.

ISBN 0 7500 1559 4

Contents

Kitchen safety

- Ask an adult to help you with hot pans and dishes and always wear oven gloves when touching hot things.
- Make sure hot things go on a mat or wooden board, not straight on to a table or a work surface.
- Be careful with sharp knives and always use a chopping board.
- Do not eat raw cake mix. It can cause stomach upsets.
- Before you do any cooking, tie back long hair, wash your hands, pull up your sleeves and put on an apron.
- Wash up and tidy up as you go along, put everything away afterwards and clear up any mess.

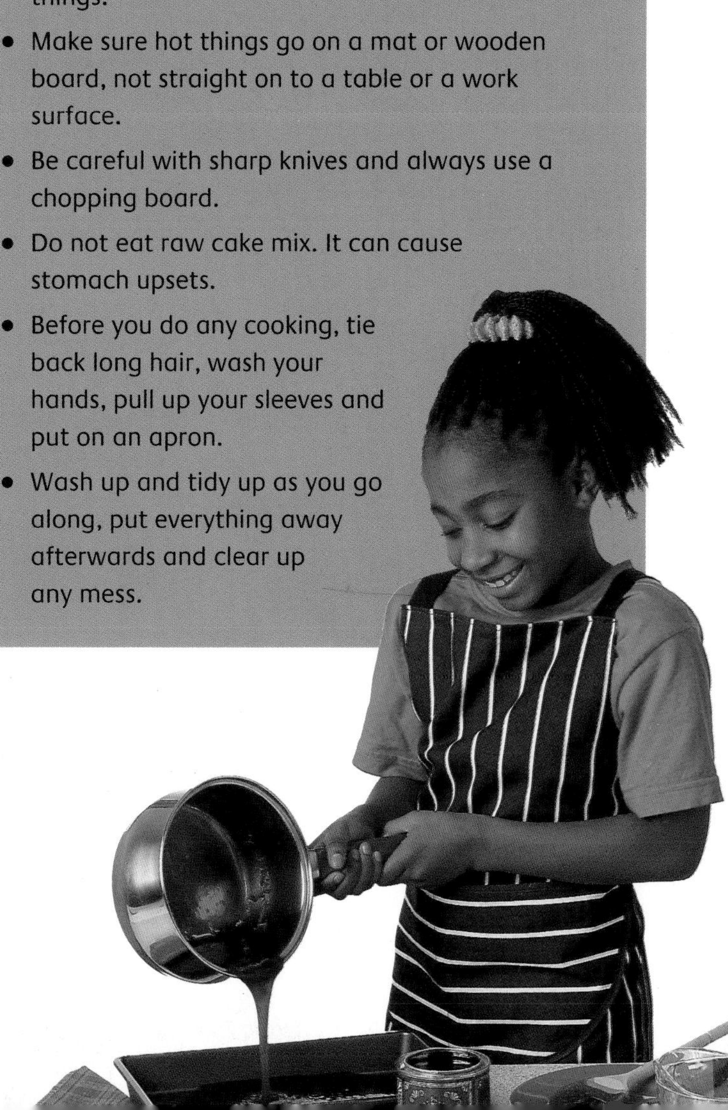

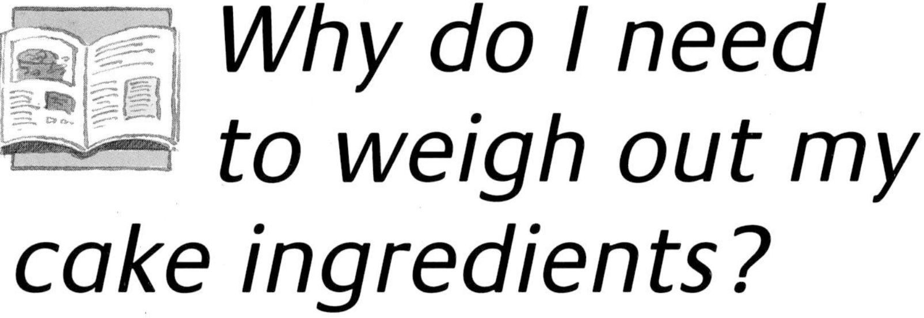

Why do I need to weigh out my cake ingredients?

When you are making a cake, it is important to use the right amount of each ingredient. Then the cake will cook properly and taste good too! Whatever you are cooking, look at a recipe to find out how much you need of each ingredient. The cooks who write the recipes try out different amounts until they find the ones that work best.

My sponge cake recipe

Ingredients

175 g butter or margarine
175 g caster sugar
175 g self-raising flour, sifted
3 large eggs
2-3 drops vanilla essence

Kitchen scales are the most accurate way to weigh dry ingredients, such as flour, sugar and butter. They measure the amount of 'stuff' the ingredients are made of. If you don't measure out ingredients, your cake may not cook properly and may taste funny!

How to make the cake

1 Set the oven to 190°C or 375°F or Gas Mark 5.
2 Mix everything together with a wooden spoon.
3 Beat the mixture as hard as you can for about two minutes.
4 Grease two 18.5 cm sandwich tins and line the bottom of each tin with greaseproof paper. Grease the paper, too.
5 Put half the mixture in each tin and bake in the oven for about 20 minutes.
6 When the cakes are cool, spread jam on one cake and put the other cake on top.

Why do I need to sift the flour?

By shaking the flour through a sieve or a flour sifter, you can get rid of any lumps. Sifting flour also helps to trap air in it, and this will make your cake lighter. Sifted flour is easier to mix with other ingredients, too.

Why do I need to grease my cake tin?

Greasing the tin with fat or oil makes a smooth surface which the cake can slide over easily. This helps to stop the cake mixture sticking to the tin as it cooks. It also makes it easier to get the cake out of the tin when it's ready.

Did you know that eggs are egg-shaped so they don't roll out of a bird's nest easily?

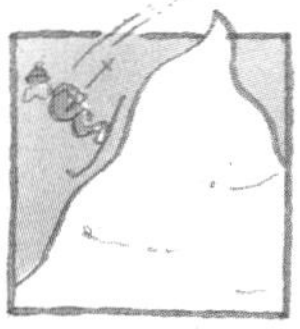

Why do egg whites go stiff when I whisk them?

Egg white - the bit around the yellow yolk - is a mixture of water and a substance called protein. Raw egg white clings together in long, sticky strings because the long chains of protein in it are wrapped around each other in neat parcels. The proteins in egg white are very delicate and when you whisk them, the chains are damaged. They unravel and become all tangled up. The tangled chains of protein trap air, forming a stiff white foam.

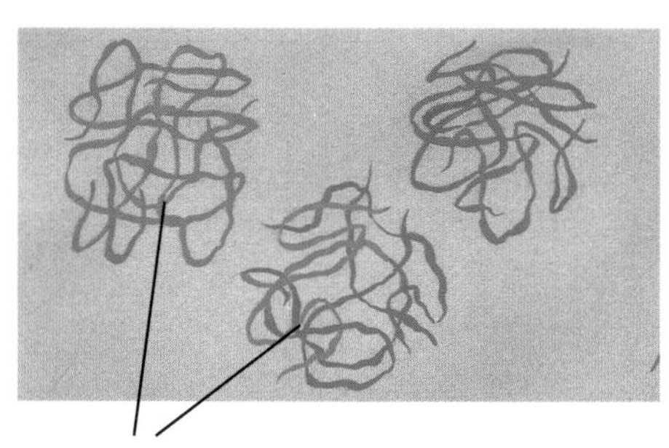

neat parcels of protein

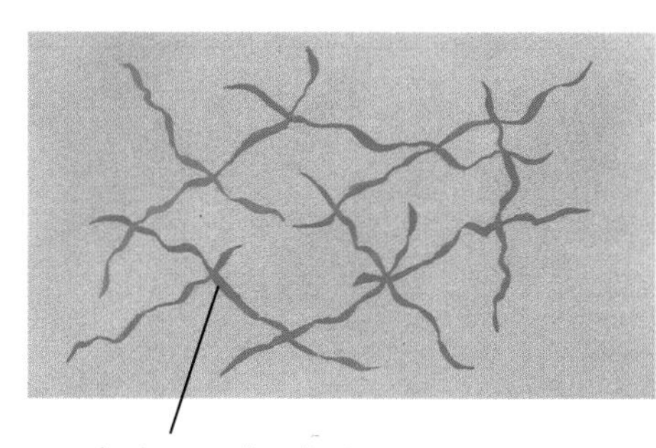

tangled protein chains

Why does yeast go frothy?

When you make some kinds of bread, you add yeast to make the bread rise. Yeast is a tiny plant that makes bubbles of carbon dioxide gas as it feeds and grows. The bubbles puff up the dough. Bread that rises a lot is called leavened bread.

Why do I knead my bread dough?

When you knead bread dough, you have to fold it and punch it down over and over again. This makes some of the wheat proteins in the flour join up to form a strong, stretchy dough. Kneading also helps to break down starch in the flour into sugar. If you add yeast, it feeds on the sugar. So kneading helps the yeast to start working. The yeast makes the dough begin to rise before it goes into the oven.

Why are chapatis flat?

Although chapatis are a type of bread, they do not contain yeast. So they have no bubbles of gas to make them rise a lot. Other breads like this are matzos and pitta bread. Another name for any flat bread is unleavened bread.

Why does my cake rise in the oven?

When you beat your cake mixture, you trap a lot of air bubbles in it. When the cake is in the oven, a gas called carbon dioxide bubbles through the cake as the baking powder disappears, or dissolves, in the liquid from the eggs. All these bubbles grow bigger as they get warmer in the oven. This puffs up the cake, making it rise.

How do oven gloves protect my hands?

Oven gloves are padded and made of a material that does not let heat though easily. It is called a good insulator. This stops the heat from hot plates and dishes getting through to your hands.

Before cooking

After cooking

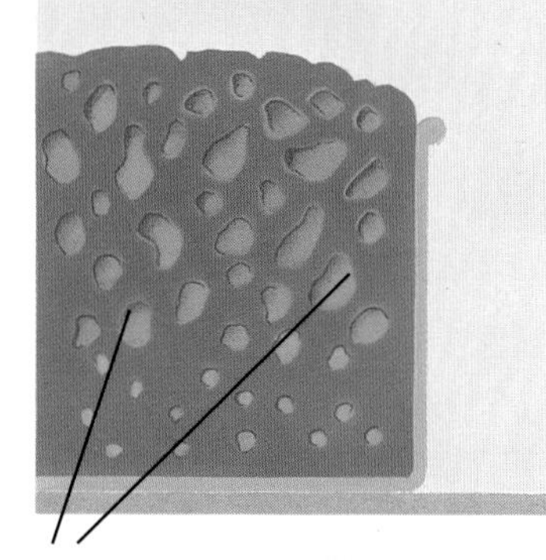

small bubbles

big bubbles

Did you know that the baking powder in self-raising flour helps cakes to rise as they cook? With plain flour, you have to add baking powder to make a cake rise.

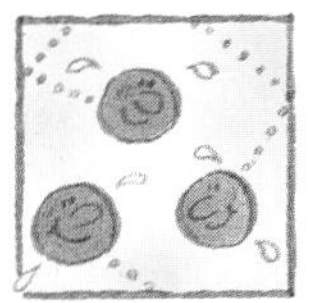

How does a microwave oven work?

Food contains tiny bits of water spread through it. Microwaves heat up food by making these tiny particles of water twist to and fro - vibrate - very fast. The water gives off heat, which cooks the food. The microwaves do not contain any heat themselves. Heat spreads through the food from the outside inwards. This movement of heat is called conduction.

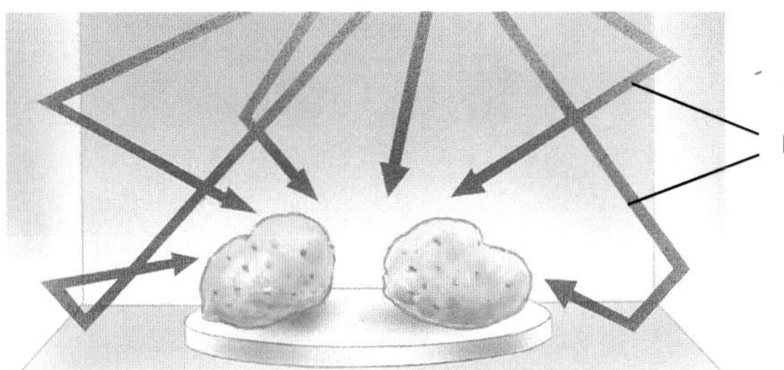

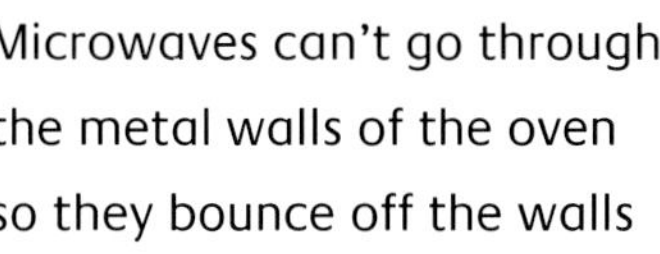

Microwaves can't go through the metal walls of the oven so they bounce off the walls on to the food.

True or false?

1 If you boil raw eggs in their shells in a microwave oven, the eggs can explode.

2 Microwave ovens heat up the food containers or plates as well as the food.

3 You can make popcorn in a microwave.

4 It's a good idea to cover foods with aluminium foil in a microwave oven.

The answers are on page 32.

Why does my popcorn pop?

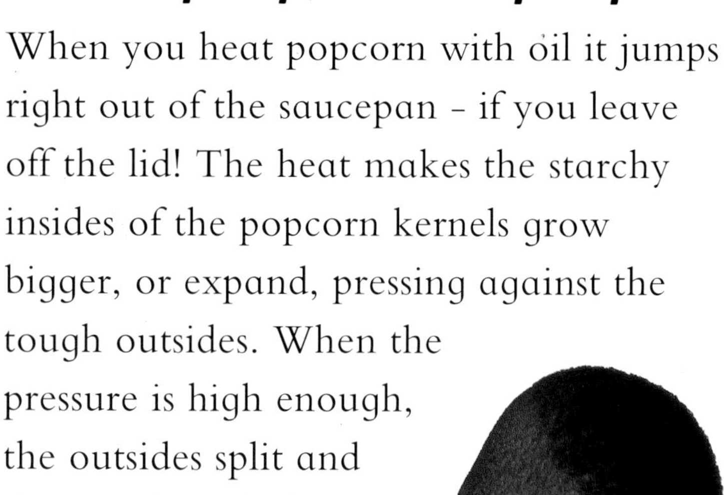

When you heat popcorn with oil it jumps right out of the saucepan - if you leave off the lid! The heat makes the starchy insides of the popcorn kernels grow bigger, or expand, pressing against the tough outsides. When the pressure is high enough, the outsides split and the starch explodes suddenly with a popping noise.

How can I clean a burnt pan?

Cover the burnt food with plenty of salt and a little water and leave it overnight. The salt should help to break up the food into smaller pieces. Then the burnt food will float off into the water, making the pan easier to clean.

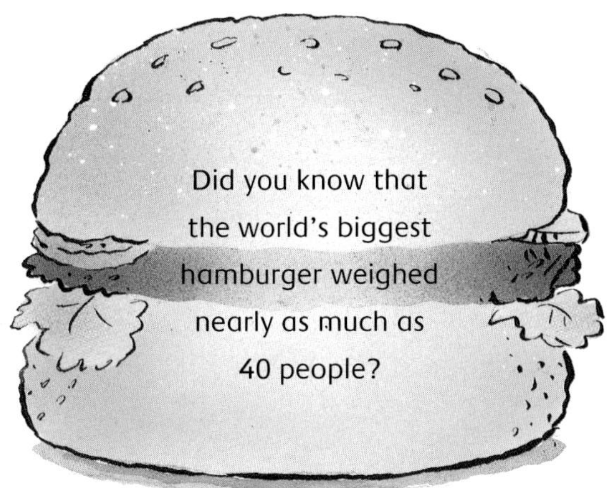

A pressure cooker cooks food very quickly by trapping steam inside. This increases the pressure enough to raise the temperature higher than the boiling point of water. Food cooks more quickly at a higher temperature – carrots cook in three or four minutes for instance – and keeps more of its goodness.

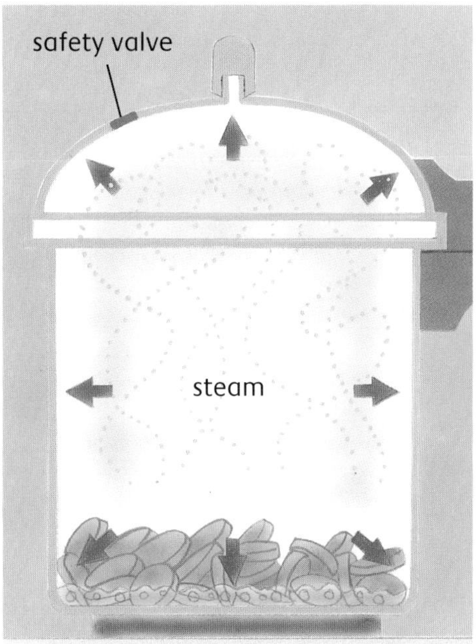

Why does my rice go soft when it's cooked?

Before you cook rice, all the little grains are too hard to eat. But when you put the rice in water and boil it, the grains go soft and grow bigger. This is because the rice soaks up the hot water, like a sponge. The same thing happens when you cook spaghetti and other sorts of pasta.

Why do my jelly cubes disappear in hot water?

In hot water, the jelly changes from solid cubes into a runny liquid. This is because the particles the jelly is made of move about very fast in the hot water. The jelly spreads through the water and disappears, or dissolves, in the water. Stirring the jelly helps it to dissolve faster.

as you stir, the jelly disappears

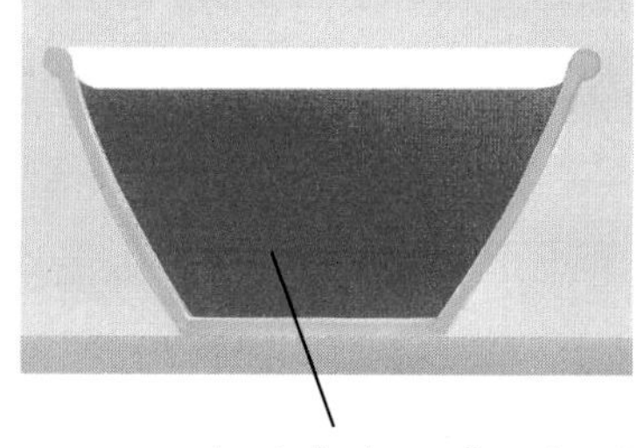

the jelly has dissolved in the water

Why does my toffee mixture go brown?

As you heat your toffee mixture, the sugar in it 'burns' to form a thick, dark brown, sticky stuff called caramel.

Why does my chocolate melt?

In solid, cool chocolate, the particles that make up the chocolate are packed tightly together and hold each other firmly in place. But when you heat the chocolate in a pan, the particles shake free and start tumbling over one another. Then the chocolate melts into a runny liquid that flows from one place to another.

Did you know that the average person eats about 1 kg of chocolate a month? That's about the same as eating a giant chocolate bar of 130 squares!

True or false?

1 The chocolate in chocolate chip biscuits does not melt when the biscuits are baked in the oven.

2 Constance Honey invented a medicine spoon made of chocolate for children.

3 Chocolate is made from the cocoa bean, which comes from a South American tree.

4 White chocolate contains milk.

The answers are on page 32.

Why should I leave my cake to cool in the tin?

If you leave your cake in the tin for a few minutes after you take it out of the oven, it will cool slightly. When things cool down, they get smaller, or contract. The cake shrinks away from the sides of the tin, which makes it come out of the tin more easily.

Did you know that a cooling rack is full of holes and so lets warmth escape into the air all around the cake? This allows the cake to cool down faster.

Why does my toffee go hard when it cools?

When you pour your hot toffee syrup on to a metal tin, it cools very suddenly. The particles of sugar in the mixture suddenly stop moving about and form a smooth, solid block of toffee. In fact the particles in the toffee are all muddled up. If they were arranged neatly, you would see crystals instead.

Why do we keep ice lollies in the freezer?

When water gets cold enough, it freezes and turns into a solid called ice. You make ice lollies by putting flavoured water into the freezer until it sets hard. If you take ice lollies out of the freezer, they will melt back to water again - unless you eat them first!

Did you know that ice cubes make drinks cool down because they take heat from the drink? Heat always goes from hotter to colder things.

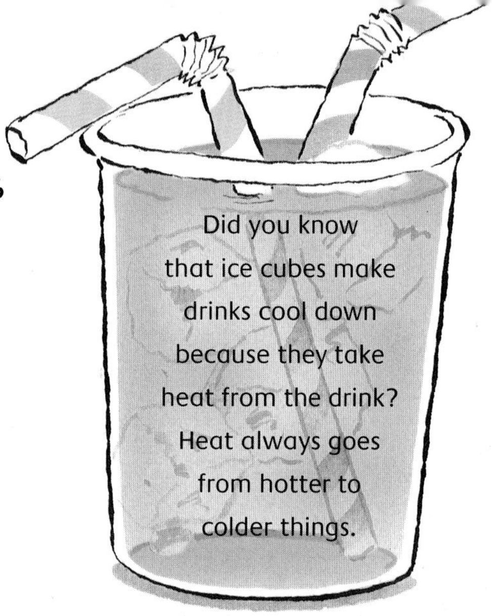

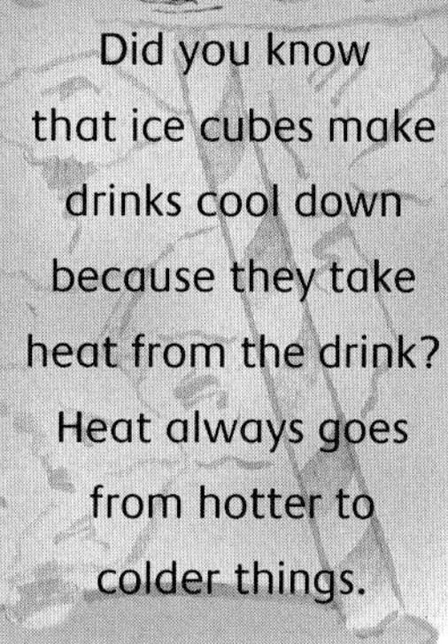

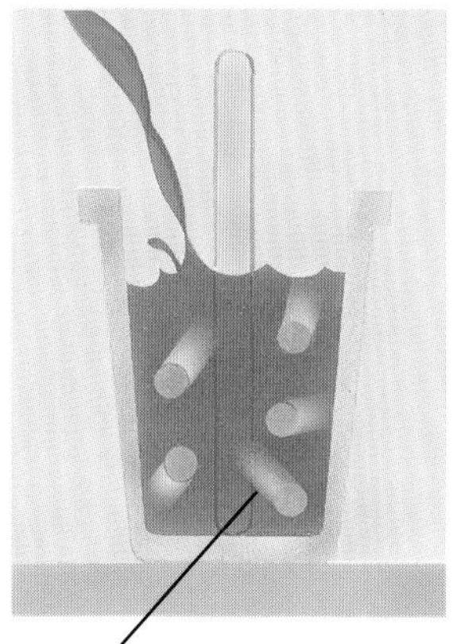

liquid – particles move about

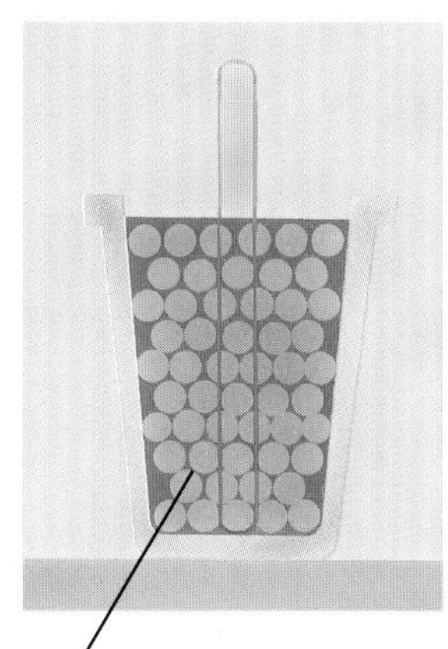

solid – particles fixed in place

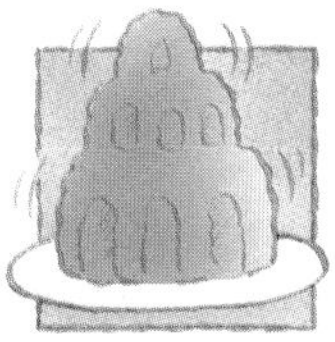

Why is jelly wobbly?

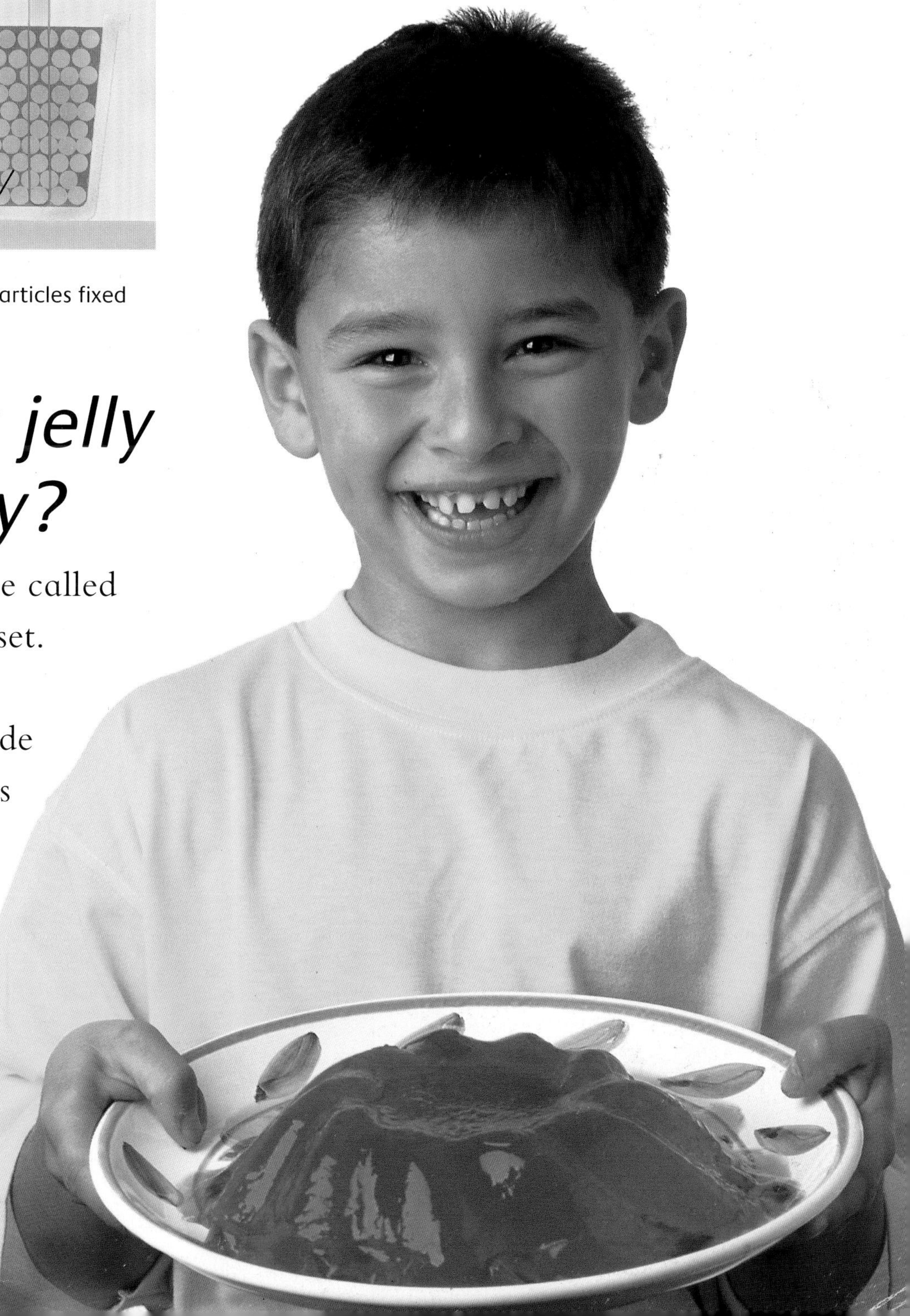

Jelly contains a substance called gelatin, which makes it set. Gelatin is tough and stretchy because it is made from the stuff that makes animal skin, bones and tendons tough and stretchy too. Gelatin also traps water, keeping the jelly wet and wobbly.

How is my ice cream made?

Ice cream is usually made from milk, sugar, eggs, cream and flavourings. The mixture is stirred and frozen at very low temperatures until it sets hard. Most of the water in the ice cream freezes into very small ice crystals. These grow larger in the freezer and can make the ice cream grainy. Stirring, or adding chemicals, helps to stop the crystals forming and keep the ice cream smooth.

Did you know that ice cream contains seaweed? Chemicals from red seaweed slow down the growth of ice crystals in the ice cream. This keeps the ice cream smooth and stops it going grainy.

What makes my milk shake light and fluffy?

Milk shakes are full of bubbles of air which are whisked into them when the ingredients are mixed together. Air is lighter than solids or liquids, so it makes milk shakes extra light and fluffy too.

Why is icing sugar so fine?

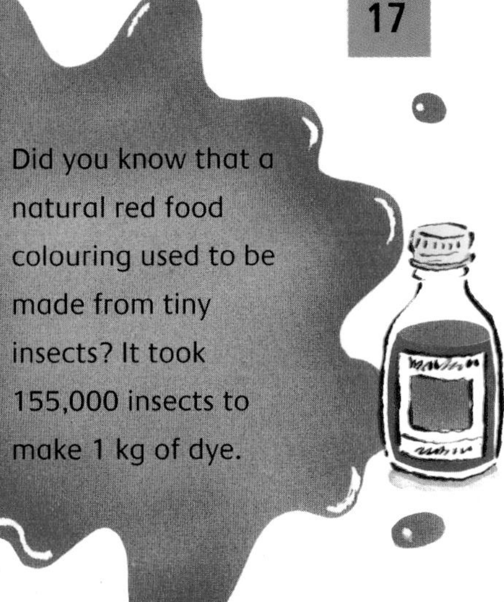

Did you know that a natural red food colouring used to be made from tiny insects? It took 155,000 insects to make 1 kg of dye.

Icing sugar is a special powdery sugar, much finer than granulated sugar or caster sugar. You cannot actually see the sugar crystals in it. This means it dissolves very quickly in water to make a smooth coating for cakes and biscuits. If you use warm water, the icing sugar will dissolve more quickly and mix more evenly with the water.

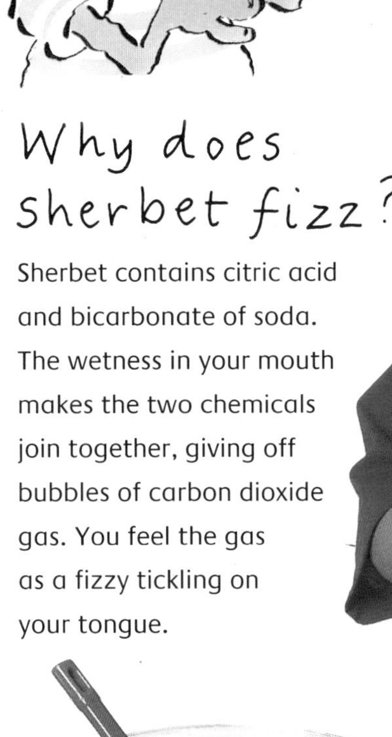

Why does sherbet fizz?

Sherbet contains citric acid and bicarbonate of soda. The wetness in your mouth makes the two chemicals join together, giving off bubbles of carbon dioxide gas. You feel the gas as a fizzy tickling on your tongue.

Why do I cry when I chop onions?

Onions contain some unusual sulphur chemicals that react with oxygen gas in the air. They form strong-smelling chemicals that irritate your eyes. Your eyes fill with tears, which wash over the surface of the eyes to get rid of the stinging chemicals. This helps to protect the delicate surface of the eyes.

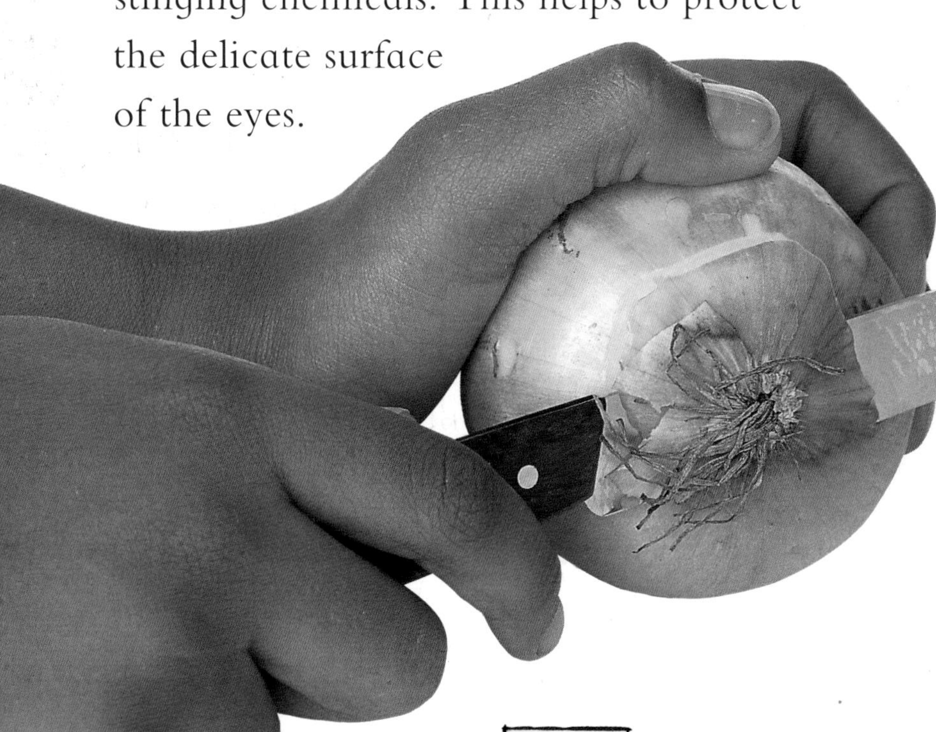

Why does lemon juice stop my cut apple going brown?

When an apple is cut open and the air can get at it, it soon turns brown. This happens when oxygen in the air joins up with with chemicals in the fruit. Substances in the fruit called enzymes make the process happen more quickly. The acid in the lemon juice slows down the work of the enzymes and helps to stop the apple going brown.

Did you know that the longest strip of peel, cut from one apple, was longer than two tennis courts?

True or false?

1 One can of cola contains seven teaspoons of sugar.

2 Peppermint tea is made from chewing gum.

3 The 'fur' in a kettle helps to keep the water warm.

The answers are on page 32.

Why do I need to shake my salad dressing?

Did you know that the largest pumpkin ever grown weighed more than two people?

Most salad dressings contain oil and vinegar. There is water in the vinegar, and oil and water do not mix. So the oil and vinegar will not mix. The oil is lighter and floats on top of the vinegar in a layer. Shaking the dressing breaks up the oil into little drops that hang in the vinegar for a while. This makes a cloudy mixture that can be used on a salad. But the layers soon separate out when the dressing is left to stand again.

Why are crisps crunchy?

Potato crisps are very thin slices of potato that are baked with fat to make them go hard. Inside a crisp are tiny pockets of air. When you bite into a crisp, the pockets of air explode and help to make the crunching sound.

Bacteria and fungi are so tiny that there are millions of them in just a tiny spot of mouldy or mushy food. As they grow, they produce spores, which are like tiny seeds. These float off into the air and start growing on other pieces of food.

mould spores

rotten lemon

Why does food sometimes go bad?

The air around you is full of tiny invisible living things called bacteria and fungi. If fresh food is not sealed up, bacteria and fungi settle on it and start to feed. They produce waste products that make the food taste and smell bad or 'off'. Some of these waste products are poisonous and make us very sick if we eat them. It's best not to touch food that has gone bad.

What are all the 'E' numbers on food labels?

The 'E' numbers that you see on food packaging are the code numbers of chemicals that are used to stop food going bad before we eat it. These chemicals are called additives. Some additives also make food taste better and keep it looking good for longer.

Why do we put food in the freezer?

When food is frozen, the bacteria and fungi in it stop growing. So food will keep in the freezer for a long time - from a month to a year - without going bad. But freezing does not kill the bacteria and fungi. So when you defrost the food, they start growing again. This is why it's best to eat frozen food on the same day you take it out of the freezer.

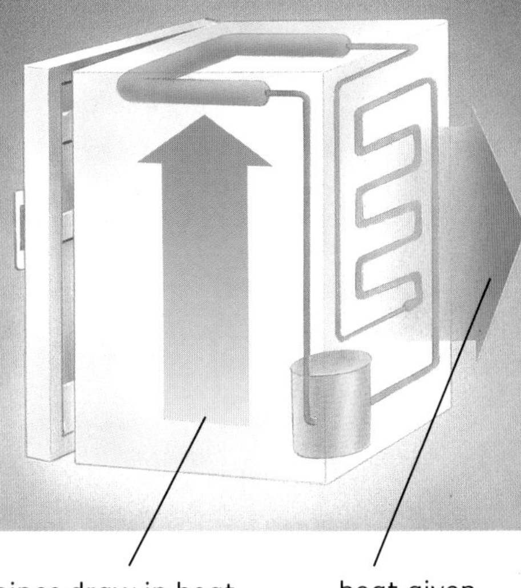

A refrigerator keeps food cold to stop it going bad. It takes heat away from the food inside and moves it to the zig-zag pipe at the back of the refrigerator. Then the air around the pipe takes away the heat from the pipe.

NASA

Did you know that astronauts eat food that is frozen and then dried? Bacteria cannot live without water so this freeze-dried food will keep at room temperature.

Did you know that tin cans were invented long before can openers? The first cans had to be opened with a hammer and chisel!

How can I turn milk into yogurt?

First you need to heat 568 ml of full-fat milk in a pan. Warm it slowly, and don't let it boil. Then pour the milk into a thermos flask or large glass jar with a screw top. Add a tablespoon of live yogurt, which is full of 'friendly' bacteria. These bacteria feed on the sugars in the milk, making it go thicker and turn into yogurt. Lastly, screw the top on the container and leave it for one or two days. If you are using a jar, keep it in a warm place, such as an airing cupboard.

What is pasteurized milk?

Pasteurized milk is heated to very high temperatures (70°C/160°F) for 15 seconds and then cooled quickly. This kills the bacteria in the milk but keeps in the flavour and the goodness. If the milk was just boiled to kill the bacteria, some of the goodness would be lost.

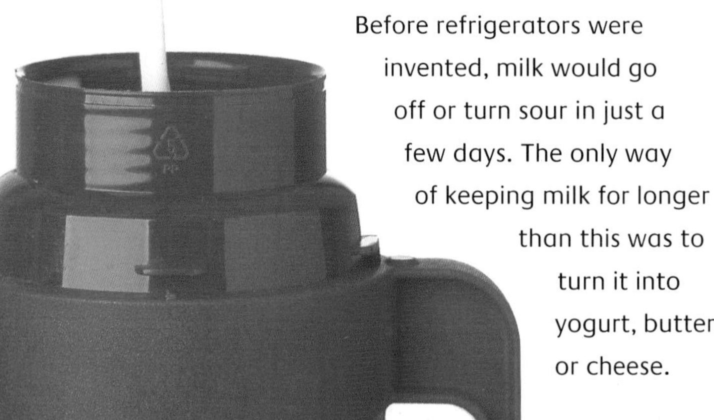

Before refrigerators were invented, milk would go off or turn sour in just a few days. The only way of keeping milk for longer than this was to turn it into yogurt, butter or cheese.

Can you spot...?

The kitchen on the left does not have a fridge or a freezer.

Can you spot five ways of making food last longer and stopping it from going off?

The answers are on page 32.

Why do raisins last for ages?

Raisins are made by drying grapes – either in the sun or using another source of heat. Most of the moisture turns into water gas and disappears, or evaporates, into the air. Bacteria and fungi need water to live and grow, so they are less likely to feed on the dry raisins. Dried fruits contain important vitamins and minerals.

Why does jam keep longer than fresh fruit?

When people make jam, they cook the fruit at high temperatures to kill the bacteria and fungi. As long as the jam is sealed in a jar, more bacteria and fungi cannot get in. So a jar of jam will keep for a long time.

How can I stop my pancake sticking to the pan?

It helps if you use a non-stick pan. These pans are coated with a special plastic called Teflon. This coating works because it does not attract other substances, and nothing sticks to its slippery surface. Also, Teflon doesn't melt when it heats up. This is why it is ideal for the inside of saucepans and cake tins. Be careful not to use metal spoons or knives in a non-stick pan. The metal may scratch off the Teflon coating.

Did you know that glass was invented by the Egyptians about 5000 years ago? It is made by heating together sand, washing soda and limestone.

Why do I stir hot pans with a wooden spoon?

Wood does not carry, or conduct, heat easily so it doesn't take in too much heat from the hot mixture in the pan. It is easy to hold the spoon while you stir. A metal spoon would draw heat from the pan and quickly get too hot to handle. This is because metal is a good conductor of heat.

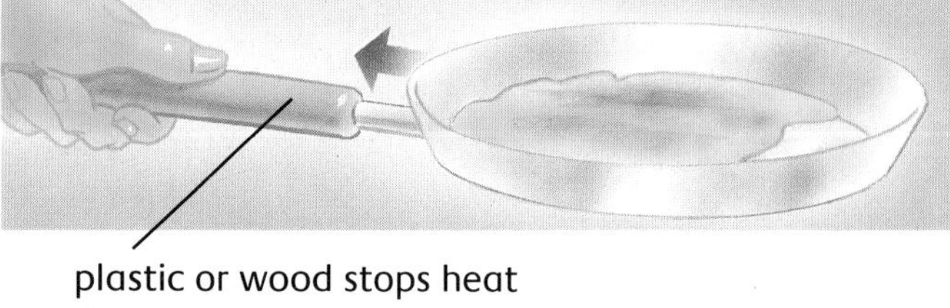

plastic or wood stops heat

metal lets heat through

Why do people sometimes cook food in tin foil?

Foil is waterproof and leakproof and it doesn't melt in a hot oven. Wrapping food in foil seals in the juices, so the food does not dry out as it cooks. Foil also keeps in the flavour of the food and keeps other smells out.

Why does clingfilm cling?

One reason is that clingfilm is elastic and can be stretched, like an elastic band. When you stop stretching it, the clingfilm tries to go back to its original shape. This creates a pulling force that makes the film stick to whatever it touches. The other reason is that clingfilm has an electrical charge which draws it towards other surfaces and makes it stick there.

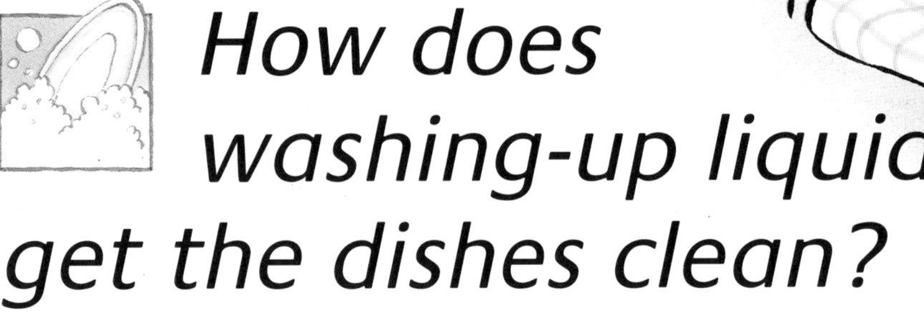

How does washing-up liquid get the dishes clean?

Washing-up liquid weakens the forces holding particles of water together. This allows water to spread more easily and helps water to mix with things better than it can on its own. The washing-up liquid also joins on to the grease on the dishes and the water clings on to the washing-up liquid. So as you brush the dishes, the grease is pulled off them.

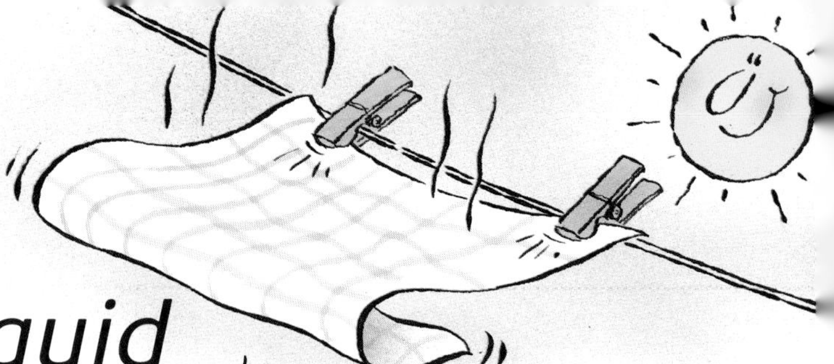

How does my drying-up cloth work?

Between the threads in your drying-up cloth, there are lots of little holes. These soak up water from the dishes and get them dry. When the cloth gets really wet, hang it somewhere warm. The warmth will turn the water into water gas, which evaporates into the air.

True or false?

1 The washing powder for automatic washing machines makes lots of bubbles.

2 If you have hard water, you need more washing-up liquid.

3 Glasses sometimes shatter in hot washing-up water.

4 Washing machines have holes inside them to keep the machine cool.

The answers are on page 32.

What is biological washing powder?

It contains some of the enzymes produced by bacteria to help them break down, or digest, their food. These enzymes attack the dirt that comes from living things, such as blood, sweat and gravy. They cut the dirt free from the cloth so that it can be washed away in the washing machine.

Why do colours sometimes run in the wash?

The colours in your clothes come from coloured chemicals called dyes, which cling to the fibres in the cloth. Most dyes stay in the cloth as long as the water isn't too hot. But at high temperatures, some of the dye can float off the cloth into the water. Then the dye can join onto other bits of cloth in the same wash.

Why is food wrapped up when you buy it?

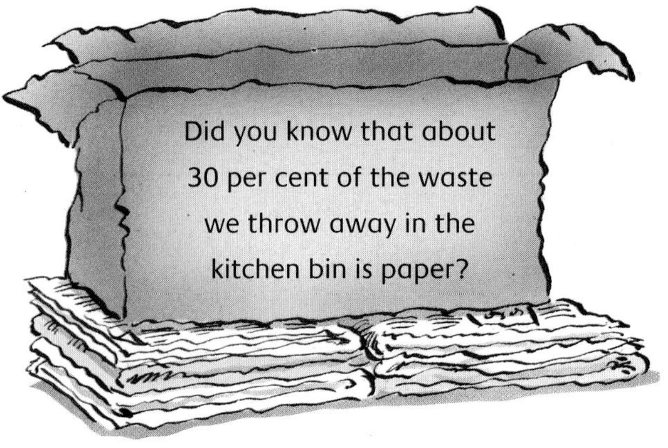

Did you know that about 30 per cent of the waste we throw away in the kitchen bin is paper?

All the paper, plastic and foil wrappings, boxes and trays around the food help to keep it fresh. They also help to stop things getting mixed up, squashed or broken and tell you what's inside. But a lot of this packaging is not really necessary. It's just there to make people buy things. Packaging fills up rubbish bins and tips very quickly. Try to choose things with less packaging and take your own carrier bags to the supermarket to save using new ones each time.

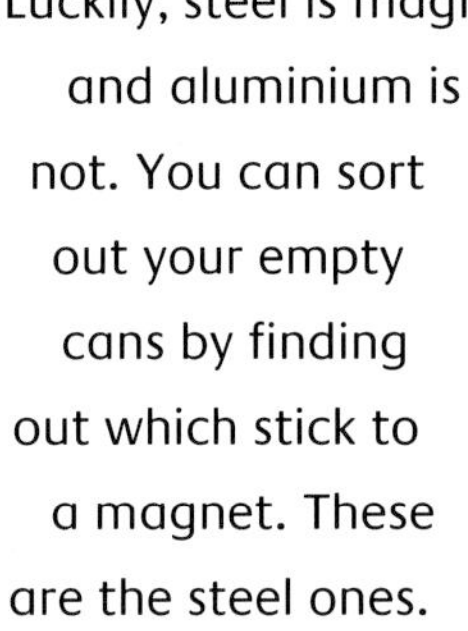

Before cans can be recycled, steel and aluminium cans have to be separated. Luckily, steel is magnetic and aluminium is not. You can sort out your empty cans by finding out which stick to a magnet. These are the steel ones.

Which kitchen waste can I recycle?

Much of the waste food you throw in the bin can be turned into compost, which can be used in your flower bed or vegetable patch. Quite a lot of other kitchen waste can be used over again and recycled in a factory to make new things. Waste paper can be mashed up and turned into new paper. Old cans and bottles can be turned into new cans and bottles. Even some plastics can be recycled.

Did you know that in one year, the average inhabitant of New York city throws away eight or nine times their own body weight in waste?

Which waste food can be turned into compost?

Vegetable peelings and leaves, apple cores, egg shells, tea and coffee grounds, and over-ripe fruit can all go on to a compost heap outside. The heap will rot down to form a compost which you can dig into the soil to make it rich and help plants grow.

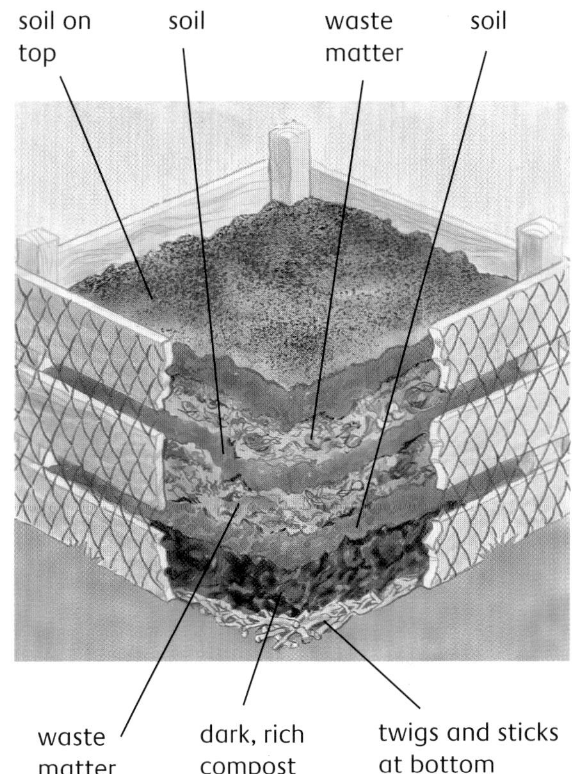

More about kitchen science

There's much more to making a cake than just cooking! From weighing and dissolving, to evaporation and recycling, all kinds of science – especially chemistry – goes on in the kitchen. Across these two pages you can read about some of the most important science ideas in this book.

Kitchen scales measure the **mass** of ingredients, which is the amount of stuff they are made of. Some scales work by balancing objects against a known mass, such as a number of kilograms.

1 Greasing baking tins cuts down a force called **friction**, which slows down or stops the movement of one surface against another.

2 **Proteins** are one of the main chemicals in living things, and are found in foods such as eggs, meat, fish, cheese and beans.

Everything is made up of tiny particles called **molecules.** Different substances are made of different molecules linked together in different ways.

3 When a substance **dissolves**, it disappears into a liquid such as water. Things dissolve faster in hot water because their molecules move about faster.

Heat is a form of energy that consists of the movement of molecules. The faster the molecules move in something, the hotter it is.

4 An **insulator** is a material that does not let heat pass through it easily.

A **conductor** is a material that does let heat pass through it easily. Pans often have wooden, plastic or ceramic handles because these do not conduct heat well. They stay cool enough for people to pick up the pan.

The movement of heat directly from hot things to cold things is called **conduction**. Heat can move through materials by conduction.

5 **Microwaves** are very short radio waves. They are a type of electric and magnetic energy that can be used for quick and easy cooking.

Pressure is the amount of force pressing on a certain area.

Temperature is how hot or cold something is.

6 Flour, rice and pasta contain **starch granules**, which swell to five times their original size in water.

7 In a **solid**, the particles, or molecules, are held tightly together and cannot move. In a **liquid**, the molecules move around freely. In a **gas**, the molecules move even faster.

8 **Contraction** means shrinking to a smaller size.

9 A **crystal** is a tiny part of a solid substance that has a regular shape because of the way its molecules are arranged in neat stacks inside. When you make sweets, if you cool the sugary mixture quickly, the sugar molecules do not have time to form crystals.

10 An **enzyme** is a protein that speeds up natural chemical reactions in living things.

Substances that can be broken down by living things are called **biodegradable**.

11 The process by which a liquid changes into a gas is called evaporation. When liquid water **evaporates**, it changes into a gas called water vapour.

An **elastic** material can stretch and then return to its original shape and size.

12 When waste materials are used again, this is called **recycling**. Recycling saves using more raw materials and uses less energy than making things from new materials.

Answers to quizzes

Page

9 **1** True. The air inside the egg heats up and expands so quickly, that the inside of the egg bursts through the shell; **2** False. Only the food is heated, so it cooks more quickly. Plates may come out hot, though, because they are heated by the hot food; **3** True; **4** False. The metal foil reflects the microwaves away from the food.

13 **1** False. The chocolate does melt, but the biscuit mixture hardens around it, so the chocolate can't spread out; **2** True. But the idea never caught on – the children ate all the spoons! **3** True; **4** False. It contains only cocoa butter with sugar and vanilla.

18 **1** True. **2** False. It is made from mint leaves; **3** False. The chalky 'fur' collects on a kettle element when water boils and turns into a gas. The water leaves behind minerals, which were dissolved in it.

23 **1** Drying – herbs, pasta and rice; **2** Bottling – jam; **3** Pickling – onions; **4** Pasteurizing – butter, cheese and yogurt; **5** Canning.

27 **1** False. If it did, bubbles would leak out of the machine and spread all over the floor; **2** True. Hard water contains lots of minerals and the washing-up liquid joins up with them so there is less to clean the dishes; **3** True. Glass conducts heat badly, so the outside of the glass heats up and expands, while the inside stays cooler. This may pull the glass apart; **4** False. The holes are there to let the water out.

Index

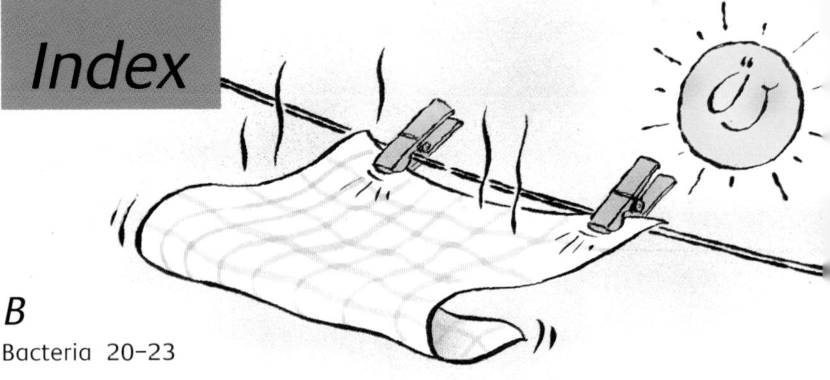